Watching the Weather

Fog and Mist

Elizabeth Miles

Heinemann
LIBRARY

www.heinemann.co.uk/library

To order:
☎ Phone 44 (0) 1865 888066
▤ Send a fax to 44 (0) 1865 314091
▢ Visit the Heinemann Bookshop at www.heinemann.co.uk/library to browse our catalogue and order online.

First published in Great Britain by Heinemann Library, Halley Court, Jordan Hill, Oxford OX2 8EJ, part of Harcourt Education.
Heinemann is a registered trademark of Harcourt Education Ltd.

Editorial: Nancy Dickmann and Daniel Cuttell
Design: Richard Parker and Q2A Solutions
Illustrations: Jeff Edwards
Picture Research: Maria Joannou and Lynda Lines
Production: Camilla Smith

Originated by Ambassador Litho Ltd.
Printed and bound in China by South China Printing Company

ISBN 0 431 19034 8
09 08 07 06 05
10 9 8 7 6 5 4 3 2 1

British Library Cataloguing in Publication Data

Miles, Elizabeth
 Fog and Mist. – (Watching the weather)
 551.5'75

A full catalogue record for this book is available from the British Library.

Acknowledgements

The Publishers would like to thank the following for permission to reproduce photographs: Alamy pp. **17** (Justin Kase), **18** (Dennis Hallinan), **25** (K-PHOTOS); Corbis pp. **5** (Tim Thompson), **6** (Owen Franken), **8** (Dick Durrance II), **9** (Dick Durrance II), **11** (Craig Tuttle), **12** (Owen Franken), **16**, **26** (Nik Wheeler); Getty Images pp. **7** (Photographer's Choice/Jonathan Gale), **13** (Image Bank/Joseph Devenney), **15** (PhotoDisc); Network pp. **22** (Jean-Claude Coutausse), **23** (Jean-Claude Coutausse); NHPA pp. **20** (Nigel J Dennis), **21** (Anthony Bannister); PA Photos p. **4** (EPA); Rex Features p. **14** (Shout); Science Photo Library pp. **24** (Dr Juerg Alean), **27** (Mark Clarke); The Weather Channel p. **16**; Tudor Photography pp. **28**, **29**.

Cover photograph of mist surrounding Jinshanling, Great Wall of China, reproduced with permission of Getty Images/Digital Vision.

The Publishers would like to thank Daniel Ogden for his assistance in the preparation of this book.

Contents

What are fog and mist? 4

What are fog and mist made of? 6

Is it foggy or misty? 8

How do fog and mist form? 10

Fog at sea 12

High and low fog 14

Fog warnings 16

Fog lights and sounds 18

Mist, plants and animals 20

Mist, fog and people 22

Disaster: freezing fog 24

Is it fog? 26

Project: making mist 28

Glossary 30

Find out more 31

Index 32

Words appearing in the text in bold, **like this**, are explained in the Glossary.

 Find out more about fog and mist at www.heinemannexplore.co.uk

What are fog and mist?

Fog and mist are clouds that lie on or near the ground. They make everything look **hazy**. Fog can be dangerous because it is difficult to see through.

In fog, drivers may turn on their headlights. This helps them to see the road ahead more easily.

Mist is easier to see through than fog.

In thick fog, you might not be able to see the other side of a road. Mist is thinner. You can see further through it.

What are fog and mist made of?

Fog and mist are made of lots of tiny water **droplets**. The droplets float in the air near the ground.

The water droplets in fog can make it difficult to see even very large objects.

The water droplets in mist are further apart. This is why it is easier to see through mist.

A tiny bit of fog or mist is made up of hundreds of water droplets. Fog feels wetter than mist because there are more water droplets in the air.

Is it foggy or misty?

It is foggy when you cannot clearly see anything more than one **kilometre** away. Fog feels wetter than mist because there are more water **droplets** in the air.

Sometimes fog is so thick you cannot see very far ahead.

Mist is less dangerous than fog because you can see more clearly ahead.

Mist is when you can clearly see everything close by. Things look **hazy** in the distance when it is misty.

How do fog and mist form?

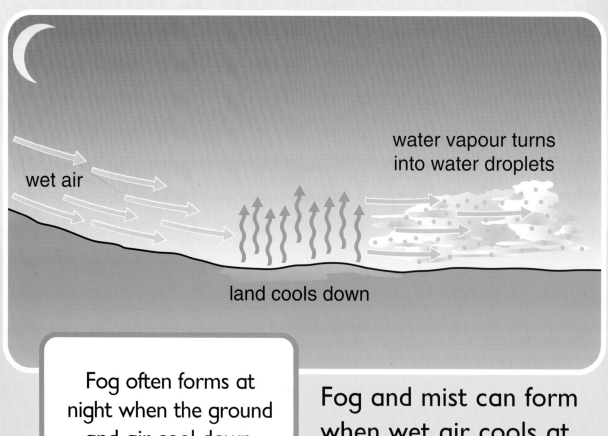

wet air

water vapour turns into water droplets

land cools down

Fog often forms at night when the ground and air cool down.

Fog and mist can form when wet air cools at night. At night, the ground often cools down the air near it. This turns **water vapour** into water **droplets**.

Mist clears when the water droplets turn back into water vapour.

During the morning, the sun warms the ground. This heats the air near the ground and any fog or mist usually clears.

Fog at sea

Fog often forms at sea. This can happen when warm, moist air passes over a colder sea.

Sea fog often fills San Francisco Bay, on the coast of the United States.

Some ships sound **foghorns** so that other ships can hear them coming.

Fog at sea can be dangerous for ships. They might sail into rocks or other ships. Ships can use **radar** to find their way in the fog.

High and low fog

On high ground where the air is cold, fog can form. Mountaineers and walkers can get lost in the fog.

Hikers cannot see the path ahead if thick fog forms.

Fog often forms near the low ground in **valleys**. This is because cool, wet air sinks below warm air and settles in the valley.

Cool, wet air in a valley can turn into thick fog.

Fog warnings

Fog can be dangerous. It is important to warn people if it might form. Car drivers may choose to stay at home if it is going to be foggy.

Weather reports sometimes warn people that fog might form.

If fog is **forecast**, signs are switched on beside motorways. They are left on until the fog clears.

5868K

Signs on motorways warn drivers to slow down because there is fog ahead.

Fog lights and sounds

Driving in fog is dangerous because it is hard to see the cars in front. Drivers turn on their headlights and fog lights.

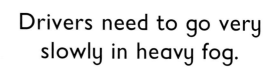

Drivers need to go very slowly in heavy fog.

Lighthouse beams are very bright. You can see them through thick fog.

In foggy weather, at night and in storms, lighthouses warn ships that land is close by. They shine a beam of light and sound a **foghorn**.

Mist, plants and animals

Plants and animals need water to live. Sometimes in hot, dry deserts, water **droplets** from mist is the only water available.

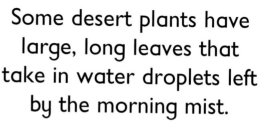

Some desert plants have large, long leaves that take in water droplets left by the morning mist.

Water runs down this beetle's back and into its mouth.

Some desert beetles collect water to drink from the early morning mist. They stand in the mist while water droplets form on their backs.

Mist, fog and people

In some dry desert areas people do not have enough water to drink. For extra water, some villages collect water from the mist or fog.

The water **droplets** from mist collect on nets and drip down into containers below.

The mist that collects on these nets is a way of getting extra water in the desert.

Water from the mist or fog is cleaned and then stored. Villagers can use the water for drinking or cooking when there is little rain.

Disaster: freezing fog

Rime is made of ice and can get very thick.

Freezing fog forms when water **droplets** in the air get very cold. The droplets are so cold that they turn into **rime** as soon as they touch a cold surface.

Passenger jets fly very high through clouds where the air can be very cold. Rime can gather on aircraft wings and can affect the controls.

Special equipment on high-flying aircraft melts the ice that can gather.

Is it fog?

In towns and cities, a **haze** that looks like fog might be smog. In smog, each water **droplet** forms on a speck of dirt in the air.

Smog is a mix of fog and smoke, or pollution.

Smog can harm our health and the **environment**. Some people try to make less **pollution**. Driving a car causes pollution, so some people cycle instead.

People sometimes wear masks so that they breathe in less smog.

Project: making mist

Now you know that mist and fog are made from water **droplets**, try making your own mist at home.

You will need:
- six or more ice cubes
- a metal plate or dish
- warm water
- a large glass or jar

1. Place the ice on the metal plate and put it in a fridge until the plate is very cold.

Ask a grown-up to help you. Ice cubes can stick to your skin!

2. Pour an inch of warm water into the bottom of the glass.

3. Quickly place the ice-cold plate on top of the glass, while the water is still warm.

4. Inside the glass, your mist will form.

Glossary

droplet very small drop of water

environment the world around us and all the living things in it

foghorn warning horn used by ships and lighthouses

forecast tells you what kind of weather might be coming

haze when things in the distance look slightly unclear, like a thin mist

kilometre measure of distance. One kilometre is the same length as about ten football pitches

pollution smoke or dirt that can damage the environment. Pollution can come from car exhausts and factory chimneys

radar equipment that uses radio waves to see objects ahead

rime kind of frost

valley low piece of land surrounded by hills

water vapour water in the air. Water vapour is a gas that we cannot see

weather report information telling you what the weather is going to be like

Find out more

More books to read

Nature's Patterns: Weather Patterns, Monica Hughes (Heinemann Library, 2004)

Nature's Patterns: Seasons, Anita Ganeri (Heinemann Library, 2004)

Seasons: Winter, Monica Hughes (Raintree, 2003)

Websites to visit

http://www.bbc.co.uk/weather/weatherwise
A website packed with information about how the weather affects us, weather images and facts, and lots of fun games, projects and activities.

http://www.onlineweather.com
Find out and see what the weather is like all around the world.

Index

aircraft 25

driving 4, 16–17, 18
droplets 6–7, 8, 10–11,
    20–21, 22, 24, 26, 28,
    30

environment 27, 30

forecast 17, 30

ground 4, 6, 10–11,
    14–15

haze 4, 9, 26, 30

pollution 26–7, 30

radar 13, 30
rime 24, 25, 30

sea 12, 13
ships 13, 19
smog 26, 27

valleys 15, 30

warm air 12, 15
wet air 10, 15